LOVE THE LOVELESS

A study on Jonah

LOVEGODGREATLY.COM

AT LOVE GOD GREATLY, YOU'LL FIND
REAL, AUTHENTIC WOMEN. WOMEN WHO
ARE IMPERFECT, YET FORGIVEN.

Women who desire less of us, and a whole lot
more of Jesus. Women who long to know God
through His Word, because we know that Truth
transforms and sets us free. Women who are
better together, saturated in God's Word and in
community with one another.

Welcome, friend. We're so glad you're here...

CONTENTS

WELCOME

We are glad you have decided to join us in this Bible study! First of all, please know that you have been prayed for! It is not a coincidence you are participating in this study.

Our prayer for you is simple: that you will grow closer to our Lord as you dig into His Word each and every day! As you develop the discipline of being in God's Word on a daily basis, our prayer is that you will fall in love with Him even more as you spend time reading from the Bible.

Each day before you read the assigned Scripture(s), pray and ask God to help you understand it. Invite Him to speak to you through His Word. Then listen. It's His job to speak to you, and it's your job to listen and obey.

Take time to read the verses over and over again. We are told in Proverbs to search and you will find: "Search for it like silver, and hunt for it like hidden treasure. Then you will understand" (Prov. 2:4–5 NCV).

All of us here at Love God Greatly can't wait for you to get started, and we hope to see you at the finish line. Endure, persevere, press on—and don't give up! Finish well what you are beginning today. We will be here every step of the way, cheering you on! We are in this together. Fight to rise early, to push back the stress of the day, to sit alone and spend time in God's Word! Let's see what God has in store for you in this study! Journey with us as we learn to love God greatly with our lives!

As you go through this study, join us in the following resources below:

Weekly Blog Posts •

Weekly Memory Verses •

Weekly Challenges •

Facebook, Twitter, Instagram •

LoveGodGreatly.com •

Hashtags: #LoveGodGreatly •

RESOURCES

Join Us

ONLINE
lovegodgreatly.com

STORE
lovegodgreatly.com/store

FACEBOOK
facebook.com/LoveGodGreatly

INSTAGRAM
instagram.com/lovegodgreatlyofficial

TWITTER
@_LoveGodGreatly

DOWNLOAD THE APP

CONTACT US
info@lovegodgreatly.com

CONNECT
#LoveGodGreatly

LOVE
GOD
GREATLY

Love God Greatly (LGG) is a beautiful community of women who use a variety of technology platforms to keep each other accountable in God's Word. We start with a simple Bible reading plan, but it doesn't stop there.

Some women gather in homes and churches locally, while others connect online with women across the globe. Whatever the method, we lovingly lock arms and unite for this purpose: to love God greatly with our lives.

Would you consider reaching out and doing this study with someone?

In today's fast-paced technology-driven world, it would be easy to study God's Word in an isolated environment that lacks encouragement or support, but that isn't the intention here at Love God Greatly. God created us to live in community with Him and with those around us.

We need each other, and we live life better together. Because of this, would you consider reaching out and doing this study with someone?

Rest assured we'll be studying right alongside you—learning with you, cheering for you, enjoying sweet fellowship, and smiling from ear to ear as we watch God unite women together—intentionally connecting hearts and minds for His glory.

So here's the challenge: call your mom, your sister, your grandma, the girl across the street, or the college friend across the country. Gather a group of girls from your church or workplace, or meet in a coffee shop with friends you have always wished you knew better.

Arm-in-arm and hand-in-hand, let's do this thing...together.

SOAP STUDY
HOW AND WHY TO SOAP

In this study we offer you a study journal to accompany the verses we are reading. This journal is designed to help you interact with God's Word and learn to dig deeper, encouraging you to slow down and reflect on what God is saying to you that day.

At Love God Greatly, we use the SOAP Bible study method. Before beginning, let's take a moment to define this method and share why we recommend using it during your quiet time in the following pages.

The most important ingredients in the SOAP method are your interaction with God's Word and your application of His Word to your life.

It's one thing to simply read Scripture. But when you interact with it, intentionally slowing down to really reflect on it, suddenly words start popping off the page. The SOAP method allows you to dig deeper into Scripture and see more than you would if you simply read the verses and then went on your merry way.

The most important ingredients in the SOAP method are your interaction with God's Word and your application of His Word to your life:

Blessed is the one who does not walk in step with the wicked or stand in the way that sinners take or sit in the company of mockers, but whose delight is in the law of the LORD, and who meditates on his law day and night. That person is like a tree planted by streams of water, which yields its fruit in season and whose leaf does not wither—whatever they do prospers. (Ps. 1:1–3, NIV)

Please take the time to SOAP through our Bible studies and see for yourself how much more you get from your daily reading.

You'll be amazed.

SOAP STUDY *(CONTINUED)*

WHAT DOES SOAP MEAN?

S STANDS FOR
SCRIPTURE

Physically write out the verses.

You'll be amazed at what God will reveal to you just by taking the time to slow down and write out what you are reading!

MONDAY

READ
Colossians 1:5–8

SOAP
Colossians 1:5–8

Scripture

WRITE
OUT THE
SCRIPTURE
PASSAGE
FOR THE
DAY.

The faith and love that spring from the hope stored up for you in heaven and about which you have already heard in the true message of the gospel that has come to you. In the same way, the gospel is bearing fruit and growing throughout the whole world just as it has been doing among you since the day you heard it and truly understood God's grace. You learned it from Epaphras, our dear fellow servant, who is a faithful minister of Christ on our behalf, and who also told us of your love in the Spirit.

Observations

WRITE
DOWN 1 OR 2
OBSERVATIONS
FROM THE
PASSAGE

When you combine faith and love, you get hope. We must remember that our hope is in heaven; it is yet to come. The gospel is the Word of truth. This gospel is continually bearing fruit and growing from the first day to the last. It just takes one person to change a whole community. Epaphras.

O STANDS FOR
OBSERVATION

What do you see in the verses that you're reading?

Who is the intended audience? Is there a repetition of words?

What words stand out to you?

A STANDS FOR **APPLICATION**

This is when God's Word becomes personal.

What is God saying to you today?

How can you apply what you just read to your own personal life?

What changes do you need to make? Is there action you need to take?

Applications

WRITE DOWN 1 OR 2 APPLICATIONS FROM THE PASSAGE.

God used one man, Epaphras, to change a whole town. I was reminded that we are simply called to tell others about Christ; it is God's job to spread the gospel, to grow it, and have it bear fruit. I felt today's verses were almost directly spoken to Love God Greatly women: The gospel is bearing fruit and growing throughout the whole world just as it has been doing among you since the day you heard it and truly understood God's grace.

Pray

WRITE OUT A PRAYER OVER WHAT YOU LEARNED FROM TODAY'S PASSAGE.

Dear Lord, please help me to be an Epaphras, to tell others about You and then leave the results in Your loving hands. Please help me to understand and apply personally what I have read today to my life, thereby becoming more and more like You each and every day. Help me to live a life that bears the fruit of faith and love, anchoring my hope in heaven, not here on earth. Help me to remember that the best is yet to come!

P STANDS FOR **PRAYER**

Pray God's Word back to Him. Spend time thanking Him.

If He has revealed something to you during this time in His Word, pray about it.

If He has revealed some sin that is in your life, confess. And remember, He loves you dearly.

A RECIPE FOR YOU

NIGERIAN MASA RECIPE (HAUSA MASA)

Prep Time: 16 hrs
Cook Time: 10 mins

Ingredients

3 Cups of rice - use The Tuwo Rice or Jasmine Rice

3 Tablespoons of pre-cooked rice

2 Teaspoons of active dry yeast

4 Tablespoons of Sugar

1 Cup of Water a little more or less + 1/4 Cup for proofing the Yeast

Vegetable Oil

Pinch of Salt

Directions

- Soak the 3 cups of rice for at least 8 hours, or better still leave overnight.

- Rinse the rice and blend it together with the 3 tablespoons of pre-cooked rice until creamy (remember to add the 1 cup of water before blending).

- Proof the yeast by mixing the yeast, sugar and ¼ cup warm water and set aside.

- Add the salt and proofed yeast to the rice mixture and mix together. The final masa mixture should have a creamy, custard-like consistency.

- Cover up the mixture for about 6 - 8 hours (you could leave it overnight as well). Use a very large bowl for this step to save you from wasting your rice and cleaning up your counters because the rice mixture will rise very high before it collapses!

- Add just a tiny bit of oil in your pan or skillet and add a pancake-size amount of masa.

- Fry both sides 2-3 minutes till golden brown (like pancakes, wait until you see small bubbles appear before you flip your cake) and serve with honey, maple syrup, hot sauce, or saya (barbecue meat) .... and ENJOY!

LGG HAUSA TESTIMONY

EBOSEREME AIFUOBHOKHAN, NIGERIA

My name is Ebosereme Aifuobhokhan, but you can call me Ebos. I am 27-years-old. I am a Nigerian and live in Nigeria. My parents are preachers and missionaries. Growing up I never wanted a part in my parents' life because I felt it was boring. I wanted the excitement and good things in life. And that led me to a wrong life until God captured my heart. During all of this, my parents never stopped praying for me.

When I started this new life with God, He gave me an insatiable appetite for His Word. I knew I was going to be a teacher of God's Word, sharing the little I knew. But there is always in our hearts a desire to do more and glorify God more with our lives. I went online looking for a study to do during a very terrible time of my life and I stumbled on Love God Greatly. But it was not an accident - God was leading me here.

God is changing one woman at a time.

I joined about 3 years ago during the 1st and 2nd Peter study. I loved every bit of it and when the next study was announced, and new facilitators were needed, I volunteered. It was scary all the way because I've never done anything like this! In my country, we are not exposed to opportunities like this. But I facilitated, and until Jesus returns, this will be the best of life.

2 years ago, my dear friend Martha asked if I would love to translate the Love God Greatly studies into a Nigerian language. Now, if you've read my story you'd know that I was under the bonds of the devil with no ambition in life and hope. Suddenly I was being told that I can lead women in God's Word and also translate and be a blessing and useful. It broke my heart with joy.

And that night I cried tears of joy. Tears that "Ebos, a Nigerian, a failure could do something Godly and productive with my life" - it was beyond me. And I've never regretted that decision to do this. Love God Greatly Nigeria is growing. God is changing one woman at a time. My life has been eternally changed because He is King, He loves women, even the young ones like me!

To connect with LGG Hausa Branch:

- facebook.com/lovegodgreatlynigeria
- Instagram: @lovegodgreatlynigeria
- Email: ebosaifuo@gmail.com

Do you know someone who could use our *Love God Greatly* Bible studies in Hausa? If so, make sure and tell them about LGG Hausa and all the amazing Bible study resources we provide to help equip them with God's Word!!!

LOVE THE LOVELESS

A study on Jonah

Let's Begin

INTRODUCTION
LOVE THE LOVELESS

We need the powerful reminder found in the book of Jonah today.

The reminder that God's salvation is for all people, no matter their history or their past sins.

We need to hear God's call again to go, go to those who are far from God and tell them about Him. We don't need to worry about whether they will respond. The book of Jonah reminds us that it's the power of the Message, not the messenger which brings people to repentance and salvation. We just need to be obedient to go and not run in the opposite direction.

You see, the story of Jonah is more than just a story of a disobedient, runaway prophet and a hungry fish.

It's a story of a compassionate God who longs for no one to die, not even a nation who has done great evil in His sight. Regardless of their sins, He still longs for them to come to salvation. His heart of compassion is not limited by the severity of their sins. He desires for them to turn from their evil ways and repent, rather than continue down their destructive roads which lead to judgement.

So, God sends one of His own, a reluctant prophet to warn them of the coming judgement.

The story of Jonah is not just a story of a compassionate God and a rebellious nation, but also the story of a compassionate God to His disobedient child. Like Jonah, God has called each of us to do things in life that we haven't wanted to do. For some, it is to forgive someone who has hurt you. For others, it is to reach out to someone not like you and show them love. Still for others, it is giving up a variety of addictions that compete for our hearts.

Whether we are an outsider to the Kingdom of God, like the people of Nineveh, or an insider, like Jonah, the book of Jonah is a reminder that God goes to great lengths to demonstrate His grace and mercy to all.

Written as a historical narrative, the book of Jonah doesn't focus on Jonah's prophecies but rather on his story of running from God and finally turning back to God in reluctant obedience. It's a story Jonah wasn't eager to participate in, yet a powerful story that shows God's sovereignty through each chapter.

Maybe like Jonah, God is calling you to reach out to someone who if far from God. Someone who might be hard to love but needs to hear about God's relentless love and salvation anyway. And maybe in your heart, you are reluctant to go, too. Go anyway and your heart will follow.

May we all seek to love the loveless in our lives.

I promise lives will be changed when we do, maybe even our own.

No one is beyond redemption.

This is a story about what God can do when people repent. It's a reminder that God is sovereign.

READING PLAN

GOD IS SOVEREIGN

Monday – God´s will vs. my will
Read: Jonah 1:1-3, Psalm 139:7-10
SOAP: Psalm 139:7-10

Tuesday - God is always in control of the weather
Read: Jonah 1:4-6, Psalm 135:5-6
SOAP: Psalm 135:5-6

Wednesday - Stop running from God and obey
Read: Jonah 1:7-12, 1 John 2:4-6
SOAP: 1 John 2:4-6

Thursday – Admit your sin and move forward
Read: Jonah 1:13-17, 1 John 1:9
SOAP: 1 John 1:9

Friday – You can't hide from God
Read: Hebrews 4:12-13
SOAP: Hebrews 4:13

GOD IS IN THE MIDST OF OUR STORMS...EVEN WHEN WE DISOBEY.

Monday - God can always hear our prayers
Read: Jonah 2:1-2, 1 John 5:14
SOAP: 1 John 5:14

Tuesday – God hears our cries for help
Read: Jonah 2:3-4, Psalm 31:22
SOAP: Psalm 31:22

Wednesday - God brings our lives out of the pit
Read: Jonah 2:5-7
SOAP: Jonah 2:6

Thursday - God responds to our gratitude
Read: Jonah 2:8-10, Psalm 50:23
SOAP: Psalm 50:23

Friday – God extends forgiveness and mercy
Read: Psalm 130:1-6
SOAP: Psalm 130:4-5

WEEK 3
POWER OF GOD'S MESSAGE

Monday - God is the giver of second chances
Read: Jonah 3:1-3, Lamentations 3:21-23
SOAP: Lamentations 3:21-23

Tuesday – God doesn't want anyone to perish
Read: Jonah 3:4-6, 2 Peter 3:9
SOAP: 2 Peter 3:9

Wednesday – God offers everlasting mercy
Read: Jonah 3:7-8, Proverbs 28:13
SOAP: Proverbs 28:13

Thursday - God is a God of compassion
Read: Jonah 3:9-10
SOAP: Jonah 3:10

Friday - God came into the world to save it, not condemn it
Read: John 3:17, Luke 19:10
SOAP: John 3:17

WEEK 4
GOD IS SLOW TO ANGER AND ABOUNDING IN STEADFAST LOVE

Monday – God is gracious to us
Read: Jonah 4:1-3
SOAP: Jonah 4:2

Tuesday - God holds the right to be angry, not us
Read: Jonah 4:4, Romans 3:23, Micah 6:8
SOAP: Romans 3:23, Micah 6:8

Wednesday - God is compassionate to us
Read: Jonah 4:5-9, Psalm 116:5, Psalm 103:10
SOAP: Psalm 116:5, Psalm 103:10

Thursday - God is more concerned about mercy than wrath
Read: Jonah 4:10-11, Romans 5:6-9
SOAP: Romans 5:6-9

Friday- God is good to all
Read: Psalm 145:8-9; Titus 2:11
SOAP: Psalm 145:8-9

YOUR
GOALS

We believe it's important to write out goals for this study. Take some time now and write three goals you would like to focus on as you begin to rise each day and dig into God's Word. Make sure and refer back to these goals throughout the next weeks to help you stay focused. You can do it!

1.

2.

3.

Signature:

Date:

WEEK 1

God is Sovereign

Whatever the Lord pleases,

he does, in heaven and on earth,

in the seas and all deeps.

PSALM 135:6

PRAYER

WRITE DOWN YOUR PRAYER REQUESTS
AND PRAISES FOR EACH DAY.

Prayer focus for this week:
Spend time praying for your family members.

MONDAY

TUESDAY

WEDNESDAY

THURSDAY

FRIDAY

CHALLENGE

You can find this listed in our Monday blog post.

MONDAY

Jonah 1:1-3

1 Now the word of the Lord came to Jonah the son of Amittai, saying, 2 "Arise, go to Nineveh, that great city, and call out against it, for their evil has come up before me." 3 But Jonah rose to flee to Tarshish from the presence of the Lord. He went down to Joppa and found a ship going to Tarshish. So he paid the fare and went down into it, to go with them to Tarshish, away from the presence of the Lord.

Psalm 139:7-10

7 Where shall I go from your Spirit?
   Or where shall I flee from your presence?
8 If I ascend to heaven, you are there!
   If I make my bed in Sheol, you are there!
9 If I take the wings of the morning
   and dwell in the uttermost parts of the sea,
10 even there your hand shall lead me,
   and your right hand shall hold me.

MONDAY

READ:
Jonah 1:1-3, Psalm 139:7-10

SOAP:
Psalm 139:7-10

Scripture

WRITE
OUT THE
SCRIPTURE
PASSAGE
FOR THE
DAY.

Observations

WRITE
DOWN 1 OR 2
OBSERVATIONS
FROM THE
PASSAGE.

Applications

WRITE
DOWN 1 OR 2
APPLICATIONS
FROM THE
PASSAGE.

Pray

WRITE OUT
A PRAYER
OVER WHAT
YOU LEARNED
FROM TODAY'S
PASSAGE.

TUESDAY
Scripture for Week 1

Jonah 1:4-6
4 But the Lord hurled a great wind upon the sea, and there was
a mighty tempest on the sea, so that the ship threatened to break
up. 5 Then the mariners were afraid, and each cried out to his
god. And they hurled the cargo that was in the ship into the sea to
lighten it for them. But Jonah had gone down into the inner part
of the ship and had lain down and was fast asleep. 6 So the captain
came and said to him, "What do you mean, you sleeper? Arise, call
out to your god! Perhaps the god will give a thought to us, that we
may not perish."

Psalm 135:5-6
5 For I know that the Lord is great,
   and that our Lord is above all gods.
6 Whatever the Lord pleases, he does,
   in heaven and on earth,
   in the seas and all deeps.

TUESDAY

READ:
Jonah 1:4-6, Psalm 135:5-6

SOAP:
Psalm 135:5-6

Scripture

WRITE
OUT THE
SCRIPTURE
PASSAGE
FOR THE
DAY.

Observations

WRITE
DOWN 1 OR 2
OBSERVATIONS
FROM THE
PASSAGE.

Applications

WRITE
DOWN 1 OR 2
APPLICATIONS
FROM THE
PASSAGE.

Pray

WRITE OUT
A PRAYER
OVER WHAT
YOU LEARNED
FROM TODAY'S
PASSAGE.

WEDNESDAY

Scripture for Week 1

Jonah 1:7-12

7 And they said to one another, "Come, let us cast lots, that we may know on whose account this evil has come upon us." So they cast lots, and the lot fell on Jonah. 8 Then they said to him, "Tell us on whose account this evil has come upon us. What is your occupation? And where do you come from? What is your country? And of what people are you?" 9 And he said to them, "I am a Hebrew, and I fear the Lord, the God of heaven, who made the sea and the dry land." 10 Then the men were exceedingly afraid and said to him, "What is this that you have done!" For the men knew that he was fleeing from the presence of the Lord, because he had told them.

11 Then they said to him, "What shall we do to you, that the sea may quiet down for us?" For the sea grew more and more tempestuous. 12 He said to them, "Pick me up and hurl me into the sea; then the sea will quiet down for you, for I know it is because of me that this great tempest has come upon you."

1 John 2:4-6

4 Whoever says "I know him" but does not keep his commandments is a liar, and the truth is not in him, 5 but whoever keeps his word, in him truly the love of God is perfected. By this we may know that we are in him: 6 whoever says he abides in him ought to walk in the same way in which he walked.

WEDNESDAY

READ:
Jonah 1:7-12, 1 John 2:4-6

SOAP:
1 John 2:4-6

Scripture

WRITE
OUT THE
SCRIPTURE
PASSAGE
FOR THE
DAY.

Observations

WRITE
DOWN 1 OR 2
OBSERVATIONS
FROM THE
PASSAGE.

Applications

WRITE
DOWN 1 OR 2
APPLICATIONS
FROM THE
PASSAGE.

Pray

WRITE OUT
A PRAYER
OVER WHAT
YOU LEARNED
FROM TODAY'S
PASSAGE.

THURSDAY
Scripture for Week 1

Jonah 1:13-17

13 Nevertheless, the men rowed hard to get back to dry land, but they could not, for the sea grew more and more tempestuous against them. 14 Therefore they called out to the Lord, "O Lord, let us not perish for this man's life, and lay not on us innocent blood, for you, O Lord, have done as it pleased you." 15 So they picked up Jonah and hurled him into the sea, and the sea ceased from its raging. 16 Then the men feared the Lord exceedingly, and they offered a sacrifice to the Lord and made vows.

17 And the Lord appointed a great fish to swallow up Jonah. And Jonah was in the belly of the fish three days and three nights.

1 John 1:9

9 If we confess our sins, he is faithful and just to forgive us our sins and to cleanse us from all unrighteousness.

THURSDAY

READ:
Jonah 1:13-17, 1 John 1:9

SOAP:
1 John 1:9

Scripture

WRITE
OUT THE
SCRIPTURE
PASSAGE
FOR THE
DAY.

Observations

WRITE
DOWN 1 OR 2
OBSERVATIONS
FROM THE
PASSAGE.

Applications

WRITE
DOWN 1 OR 2
APPLICATIONS
FROM THE
PASSAGE.

Pray

WRITE OUT
A PRAYER
OVER WHAT
YOU LEARNED
FROM TODAY'S
PASSAGE.

FRIDAY
Scripture for Week 1

Hebrews 4:12-13
12 For the word of God is living and active, sharper than any two-edged sword, piercing to the division of soul and of spirit, of joints and of marrow, and discerning the thoughts and intentions of the heart. 13 And no creature is hidden from his sight, but all are naked and exposed to the eyes of him to whom we must give account.

FRIDAY

READ:
Hebrews 4:12-13

SOAP:
Hebrews 4:13

Scripture

WRITE
OUT THE
SCRIPTURE
PASSAGE
FOR THE
DAY.

Observations

WRITE
DOWN 1 OR 2
OBSERVATIONS
FROM THE
PASSAGE.

Applications

WRITE
DOWN 1 OR 2
APPLICATIONS
FROM THE
PASSAGE.

Pray

WRITE OUT
A PRAYER
OVER WHAT
YOU LEARNED
FROM TODAY'S
PASSAGE.

REFLECTION QUESTIONS

1. What did God tell Jonah to do? Is there a way to run from God and His commands?

2. Sometimes, we forget we are not in control of our lives. How can we see God in control in Jonah's journey?

3. Think about the things God is asking you to do right now. Are you obeying Him or trying to run away?

4. How can we move forward when we sin and disobey God?

5. Knowing that we all are "naked" to the eyes of God, how should that affect the way we live?

NOTES

WEEK 2

*God is in the midst of our storms...
even when we disobey.*

---

*When my life was fainting away,
I remembered the LORD,
and my prayer came to you,
into your holy temple.*

JONAH 2:7

PRAYER

Prayer focus for this week:
Spend time praying for your country.

MONDAY

TUESDAY

WEDNESDAY

THURSDAY

FRIDAY

CHALLENGE

You can find this listed in our Monday blog post.

MONDAY
Scripture for Week 2

Jonah 2:1-2
1 Then Jonah prayed to the Lord his God from the belly of the fish, 2 saying,
"I called out to the Lord, out of my distress,
    and he answered me;
out of the belly of Sheol I cried,
    and you heard my voice.

1 John 5:14
14 And this is the confidence that we have toward him, that if we ask anything according to his will he hears us.

MONDAY

READ:
Jonah 2:1-2, 1 John 5:14

SOAP:
1 John 5:14

Scripture

WRITE
OUT THE
SCRIPTURE
PASSAGE
FOR THE
DAY.

Observations

WRITE
DOWN 1 OR 2
OBSERVATIONS
FROM THE
PASSAGE.

Applications

WRITE
DOWN 1 OR 2
APPLICATIONS
FROM THE
PASSAGE.

Pray

WRITE OUT
A PRAYER
OVER WHAT
YOU LEARNED
FROM TODAY'S
PASSAGE.

TUESDAY
Scripture for Week 2

Jonah 2:3-4
3 For you cast me into the deep,
   into the heart of the seas,
   and the flood surrounded me;
all your waves and your billows
   passed over me.
4 Then I said, 'I am driven away
   from your sight;
yet I shall again look
   upon your holy temple.'

Psalm 31:22
22 I had said in my alarm,
   "I am cut off from your sight."
But you heard the voice of my pleas for mercy
   when I cried to you for help.

TUESDAY

READ:
Jonah 2:3-4, Psalm 31:22

SOAP:
Psalm 31:22

Scripture

WRITE
OUT THE
SCRIPTURE
PASSAGE
FOR THE
DAY.

Observations

WRITE
DOWN 1 OR 2
OBSERVATIONS
FROM THE
PASSAGE.

Applications

WRITE
DOWN 1 OR 2
APPLICATIONS
FROM THE
PASSAGE.

Pray

WRITE OUT
A PRAYER
OVER WHAT
YOU LEARNED
FROM TODAY'S
PASSAGE.

WEDNESDAY
Scripture for Week 2

Jonah 2:5-7
5 The waters closed in over me to take my life;
　　the deep surrounded me;
weeds were wrapped about my head
6　at the roots of the mountains.
I went down to the land
　　whose bars closed upon me forever;
yet you brought up my life from the pit,
　　O Lord my God.
7 When my life was fainting away,
　　I remembered the Lord,
and my prayer came to you,
　　into your holy temple.

WEDNESDAY

READ:
Jonah 2:5-7

SOAP:
Jonah 2:6

Scripture

WRITE
OUT THE
SCRIPTURE
PASSAGE
FOR THE
DAY.

Observations

WRITE
DOWN 1 OR 2
OBSERVATIONS
FROM THE
PASSAGE.

Applications

WRITE
DOWN 1 OR 2
APPLICATIONS
FROM THE
PASSAGE.

Pray

WRITE OUT
A PRAYER
OVER WHAT
YOU LEARNED
FROM TODAY'S
PASSAGE.

THURSDAY
Scripture for Week 2

Jonah 2:8-10

8 Those who pay regard to vain idols
   forsake their hope of steadfast love.
9 But I with the voice of thanksgiving
   will sacrifice to you;
what I have vowed I will pay.
   Salvation belongs to the Lord!"
10 And the Lord spoke to the fish, and it vomited Jonah out upon
the dry land.

Psalm 50:23

23 The one who offers thanksgiving as his sacrifice glorifies me;
   to one who orders his way rightly
   I will show the salvation of God!"

THURSDAY

READ:
Jonah 2:8-10, Psalm 50:23

SOAP:
Psalm 50:23

Scripture

WRITE
OUT THE
SCRIPTURE
PASSAGE
FOR THE
DAY.

Observations

WRITE
DOWN 1 OR 2
OBSERVATIONS
FROM THE
PASSAGE.

Applications

WRITE
DOWN 1 OR 2
APPLICATIONS
FROM THE
PASSAGE.

Pray

WRITE OUT
A PRAYER
OVER WHAT
YOU LEARNED
FROM TODAY'S
PASSAGE.

FRIDAY

Scripture for Week 2

Psalm 130:1-6

1 Out of the depths I cry to you, O Lord!

2 O Lord, hear my voice!
Let your ears be attentive
  to the voice of my pleas for mercy!

3 If you, O Lord, should mark iniquities,
  O Lord, who could stand?

4 But with you there is forgiveness,
  that you may be feared.

5 I wait for the Lord, my soul waits,
  and in his word I hope;

6 my soul waits for the Lord
  more than watchmen for the morning,
  more than watchmen for the morning.

FRIDAY

READ:
Psalm 130:1-6

SOAP:
Psalm 130:4-5

Scripture

WRITE
OUT THE
SCRIPTURE
PASSAGE
FOR THE
DAY.

Observations

WRITE
DOWN 1 OR 2
OBSERVATIONS
FROM THE
PASSAGE.

Applications

WRITE
DOWN 1 OR 2
APPLICATIONS
FROM THE
PASSAGE.

Pray

WRITE OUT
A PRAYER
OVER WHAT
YOU LEARNED
FROM TODAY'S
PASSAGE.

REFLECTION QUESTIONS

1. What happens when we cry out to the Lord? How does this affect our prayer life?

2. Look up Scriptures that reassure you of the truth that God hears your pleas for mercy.

3. Can you remember a time when God brought you from the deepest pit? How did God work things out for your good and His glory?

4. How do we (like Jonah in vs 9) sacrifice to the Lord with thanksgiving? Why is it hard?

5. How can God's Word be our hope in a practical way?

NOTES

WEEK 3

Power of God's Message

Whoever conceals his transgressions will not prosper, but he who confesses and forsakes them will obtain mercy.

PROVERBS 28:13

PRAYER

WRITE DOWN YOUR PRAYER REQUESTS
AND PRAISES FOR EACH DAY.

Prayer focus for this week:
Spend time praying for your friends.

MONDAY

TUESDAY

WEDNESDAY

THURSDAY

FRIDAY

CHALLENGE

You can find this listed in our Monday blog post.

MONDAY
Scripture for Week 3

Jonah 3:1-3

1 Then the word of the Lord came to Jonah the second time, saying, 2 "Arise, go to Nineveh, that great city, and call out against it the message that I tell you." 3 So Jonah arose and went to Nineveh, according to the word of the Lord. Now Nineveh was an exceedingly great city, three days' journey in breadth.

Lamentations 3:21-23

21 But this I call to mind,
   and therefore I have hope:
22 The steadfast love of the Lord never ceases;
   his mercies never come to an end;
23 they are new every morning;
   great is your faithfulness.

MONDAY

READ:
Jonah 3:1-3, Lamentations 3:21-23

SOAP:
Lamentations 3:21-23

Scripture

WRITE
OUT THE
SCRIPTURE
PASSAGE
FOR THE
DAY.

Observations

WRITE
DOWN 1 OR 2
OBSERVATIONS
FROM THE
PASSAGE.

Applications

WRITE
DOWN 1 OR 2
APPLICATIONS
FROM THE
PASSAGE.

Pray

WRITE OUT
A PRAYER
OVER WHAT
YOU LEARNED
FROM TODAY'S
PASSAGE.

TUESDAY
Scripture for Week 3

Jonah 3:4-6
4 Jonah began to go into the city, going a day's journey.
And he called out, "Yet forty days, and Nineveh shall be
overthrown!" 5 And the people of Nineveh believed God. They
called for a fast and put on sackcloth, from the greatest of them to
the least of them.

6 The word reached the king of Nineveh, and he arose from his
throne, removed his robe, covered himself with sackcloth, and sat in
ashes.

2 Peter 3:9
9 The Lord is not slow to fulfill his promise as some count slowness,
but is patient toward you, not wishing that any should perish,
but that all should reach repentance.

TUESDAY

READ:
Jonah 3:4-6, 2 Peter 3:9

SOAP:
2 Peter 3:9

Scripture

WRITE
OUT THE
SCRIPTURE
PASSAGE
FOR THE
DAY.

Observations

WRITE
DOWN 1 OR 2
OBSERVATIONS
FROM THE
PASSAGE.

Applications

WRITE
DOWN 1 OR 2
APPLICATIONS
FROM THE
PASSAGE.

Pray

WRITE OUT
A PRAYER
OVER WHAT
YOU LEARNED
FROM TODAY'S
PASSAGE.

WEDNESDAY

Scripture for Week 3

Jonah 3:7-8

7 And he issued a proclamation and published through
Nineveh, "By the decree of the king and his nobles: Let neither man
nor beast, herd nor flock, taste anything. Let them not feed or drink
water, 8 but let man and beast be covered with sackcloth, and let
them call out mightily to God. Let everyone turn from his evil way
and from the violence that is in his hands.

Proverbs 28:13

13 Whoever conceals his transgressions will not prosper,
    but he who confesses and forsakes them will obtain mercy.

WEDNESDAY

READ:
Jonah 3:7-8, Proverbs 28:13

SOAP:
Proverbs 28:13

Scripture

WRITE
OUT THE
SCRIPTURE
PASSAGE
FOR THE
DAY.

Observations

WRITE
DOWN 1 OR 2
OBSERVATIONS
FROM THE
PASSAGE.

Applications

WRITE
DOWN 1 OR 2
APPLICATIONS
FROM THE
PASSAGE.

Pray

WRITE OUT
A PRAYER
OVER WHAT
YOU LEARNED
FROM TODAY'S
PASSAGE.

THURSDAY
Scripture for Week 3

Jonah 3:9-10

9 Who knows? God may turn and relent and turn from his fierce anger, so that we may not perish."

10 When God saw what they did, how they turned from their evil way, God relented of the disaster that he had said he would do to them, and he did not do it.

THURSDAY

READ:
Jonah 3:9-10

SOAP:
Jonah 3:10

Scripture

WRITE
OUT THE
SCRIPTURE
PASSAGE
FOR THE
DAY.

Observations

WRITE
DOWN 1 OR 2
OBSERVATIONS
FROM THE
PASSAGE.

Applications

WRITE
DOWN 1 OR 2
APPLICATIONS
FROM THE
PASSAGE.

Pray

WRITE OUT
A PRAYER
OVER WHAT
YOU LEARNED
FROM TODAY'S
PASSAGE.

FRIDAY
Scripture for Week 3

John 3:17
17 For God did not send his Son into the world to condemn the world, but in order that the world might be saved through him.

Luke 19:10
10 For the Son of Man came to seek and to save the lost."

FRIDAY

READ:
John 3:17, Luke 19:10

SOAP:
John 3:17

Scripture

WRITE
OUT THE
SCRIPTURE
PASSAGE
FOR THE
DAY.

Observations

WRITE
DOWN 1 OR 2
OBSERVATIONS
FROM THE
PASSAGE.

Applications

WRITE
DOWN 1 OR 2
APPLICATIONS
FROM THE
PASSAGE.

Pray

WRITE OUT
A PRAYER
OVER WHAT
YOU LEARNED
FROM TODAY'S
PASSAGE.

REFLECTION QUESTIONS

1. God's love never ceases. His mercy never comes to an end. In which areas of your life do you need to feel His love and mercy?

2. Think about all the people around you who don't know Jesus. Pray for their repentance and think of ways to share Jesus with them.

3. What sins do you need to confess in order to obtain God's mercy?

4. How does God respond to Nineveh's repentance?

5. Why did God send His Son into the world?

NOTES

WEEK 4

God is slow to anger and abounding in steadfast love

The *LORD* is gracious and merciful, slow to anger and abounding in steadfast love.

PSALM 145:8

PRAYER

WRITE DOWN YOUR PRAYER REQUESTS
AND PRAISES FOR EACH DAY.

Prayer focus for this week:
Spend time praying for your church.

MONDAY

TUESDAY

WEDNESDAY

THURSDAY

FRIDAY

CHALLENGE

You can find this listed in our Monday blog post.

MONDAY
Scripture for Week 4

Jonah 4:1-3

1 But it displeased Jonah exceedingly, and he was angry. 2 And he prayed to the Lord and said, "O Lord, is not this what I said when I was yet in my country? That is why I made haste to flee to Tarshish; for I knew that you are a gracious God and merciful, slow to anger and abounding in steadfast love, and relenting from disaster. 3 Therefore now, O Lord, please take my life from me, for it is better for me to die than to live."

MONDAY

READ:
Jonah 4:1-3

SOAP:
Jonah 4:2

Scripture

WRITE
OUT THE
SCRIPTURE
PASSAGE
FOR THE
DAY.

Observations

WRITE
DOWN 1 OR 2
OBSERVATIONS
FROM THE
PASSAGE.

Applications

WRITE
DOWN 1 OR 2
APPLICATIONS
FROM THE
PASSAGE.

Pray

WRITE OUT
A PRAYER
OVER WHAT
YOU LEARNED
FROM TODAY'S
PASSAGE.

TUESDAY
Scripture for Week 4

Jonah 4:4
4 And the Lord said, "Do you do well to be angry?"

Romans 3:23
23 for all have sinned and fall short of the glory of God,

Micah 6:8
8 He has told you, O man, what is good;
  and what does the Lord require of you
but to do justice, and to love kindness,
  and to walk humbly with your God?

TUESDAY

READ:
Jonah 4:4, Romans 3:23, Micah 6:8

SOAP:
Romans 3:23, Micah 6:8

Scripture

WRITE
OUT THE
SCRIPTURE
PASSAGE
FOR THE
DAY.

Observations

WRITE
DOWN 1 OR 2
OBSERVATIONS
FROM THE
PASSAGE.

Applications

WRITE
DOWN 1 OR 2
APPLICATIONS
FROM THE
PASSAGE.

Pray

WRITE OUT
A PRAYER
OVER WHAT
YOU LEARNED
FROM TODAY'S
PASSAGE.

WEDNESDAY

Scripture for Week 4

Jonah 4:5-9

5 Jonah went out of the city and sat to the east of the city and made a booth for himself there. He sat under it in the shade, till he should see what would become of the city. 6 Now the Lord God appointed a plant and made it come up over Jonah, that it might be a shade over his head, to save him from his discomfort. So Jonah was exceedingly glad because of the plant. 7 But when dawn came up the next day, God appointed a worm that attacked the plant, so that it withered. 8 When the sun rose, God appointed a scorching east wind, and the sun beat down on the head of Jonah so that he was faint. And he asked that he might die and said, "It is better for me to die than to live." 9 But God said to Jonah, "Do you do well to be angry for the plant?" And he said, "Yes, I do well to be angry, angry enough to die."

Psalm 116:5

5 Gracious is the Lord, and righteous;
  our God is merciful.

Psalm 103:10

10 He does not deal with us according to our sins,
  nor repay us according to our iniquities.

WEDNESDAY

READ:
Jonah 4:5-9, Psalm 116:5, Psalm 103:10

SOAP:
Psalm 116:5, Psalm 103:10

Scripture

WRITE
OUT THE
SCRIPTURE
PASSAGE
FOR THE
DAY.

Observations

WRITE
DOWN 1 OR 2
OBSERVATIONS
FROM THE
PASSAGE.

Applications

WRITE
DOWN 1 OR 2
APPLICATIONS
FROM THE
PASSAGE.

Pray

WRITE OUT
A PRAYER
OVER WHAT
YOU LEARNED
FROM TODAY'S
PASSAGE.

THURSDAY
Scripture for Week 4

Jonah 4:10-11
10 And the Lord said, "You pity the plant, for which you did not labor, nor did you make it grow, which came into being in a night and perished in a night. 11 And should not I pity Nineveh, that great city, in which there are more than 120,000 persons who do not know their right hand from their left, and also much cattle?"

Romans 5:6-9
6 For while we were still weak, at the right time Christ died for the ungodly. 7 For one will scarcely die for a righteous person—though perhaps for a good person one would dare even to die— 8 but God shows his love for us in that while we were still sinners, Christ died for us. 9 Since, therefore, we have now been justified by his blood, much more shall we be saved by him from the wrath of God.

THURSDAY

READ:
Jonah 4:10-11, Romans 5:6-9

SOAP:
Romans 5:6-9

Scripture

WRITE
OUT THE
SCRIPTURE
PASSAGE
FOR THE
DAY.

Observations

WRITE
DOWN 1 OR 2
OBSERVATIONS
FROM THE
PASSAGE.

Applications

WRITE
DOWN 1 OR 2
APPLICATIONS
FROM THE
PASSAGE.

Pray

WRITE OUT
A PRAYER
OVER WHAT
YOU LEARNED
FROM TODAY'S
PASSAGE.

FRIDAY
Scripture for Week 4

Psalm 145:8-9

8 The Lord is gracious and merciful,
   slow to anger and abounding in steadfast love.
9 The Lord is good to all,
   and his mercy is over all that he has made.

Titus 2:11

11 For the grace of God has appeared, bringing salvation for all
people,

FRIDAY

READ:
Psalm 145:8-9; Titus 2:11

SOAP:
Psalm 145:8-9

Scripture

WRITE
OUT THE
SCRIPTURE
PASSAGE
FOR THE
DAY.

Observations

WRITE
DOWN 1 OR 2
OBSERVATIONS
FROM THE
PASSAGE.

Applications

WRITE
DOWN 1 OR 2
APPLICATIONS
FROM THE
PASSAGE.

Pray

WRITE OUT
A PRAYER
OVER WHAT
YOU LEARNED
FROM TODAY'S
PASSAGE.

REFLECTION QUESTIONS

1. Jonah is not happy about the way the people responded. Why do you think Jonah is unhappy about the people repenting and turning to the Lord?

2. How do we sometimes act like Jonah in Chapter 4?

3. What lesson is Jonah supposed to learn from the plant (Jonah 4:5-11)? What can we learn about compassion from these verses?

4. Jesus died for us while we were still sinners. What attitude should we have towards unbelievers?

5. List the ways in which God is exceedingly gracious to sinners. How has He been gracious to you?

NOTES

KNOW THESE TRUTHS

from God's Word

God loves you.

Even when you're feeling unworthy and like the world is stacked against you, God loves you - yes, you - and He has created you for great purpose.

God's Word says, "God so loved the world that He gave His one and only Son, Jesus, that whoever believes in Him shall not perish, but have eternal life" (John 3:16).

Our sin separates us from God.

We are all sinners by nature and by choice, and because of this we are separated from God, who is holy.

God's Word says, "All have sinned and fall short of the glory of God" (Romans 3:23).

Jesus died so that you might have life.

The consequence of sin is death, but your story doesn't have to end there! God's free gift of salvation is available to us because Jesus took the penalty for our sin when He died on the cross.

God's Word says, "For the wages of sin is death, but the free gift of God is eternal life in Christ Jesus our Lord" (Romans 6:23); "God demonstrates His own love toward us, in that while we were yet sinners, Christ died for us" (Romans 5:8).

Jesus lives!

Death could not hold Him, and three days after His body was placed in the tomb Jesus rose again, defeating sin and death forever! He lives today in heaven and is preparing a place in eternity for all who believe in Him.

God's Word says, "In my Father's house are many rooms. If it were not so, would I have told you that I go to prepare a place for you? And if I go and prepare a place for you, I will come again and will take you to myself, that where I am you may be also" (John 14:2-3).

Yes, you can KNOW that you are forgiven.
Accept Jesus as the only way to salvation...

Accepting Jesus as your Savior is not about what you can do, but rather about having faith in what Jesus has already done. It takes recognizing that you are a sinner, believing that Jesus died for your sins, and asking for forgiveness by placing your full trust in Jesus's work on the cross on your behalf.

God's Word says, "If you confess with your mouth that Jesus is Lord and believe in your heart that God raised him from the dead, you will be saved. For with the heart one believes and is justified, and with the mouth one confesses and is saved" (Romans 10:9-10).

Practically, what does that look like?
With a sincere heart, you can pray a simple prayer like this:

God,
I know that I am a sinner.
I don't want to live another day without embracing
the love and forgiveness that You have for me.
I ask for Your forgiveness.
I believe that You died for my sins and rose from the dead.
I surrender all that I am and ask You to be Lord of my life.
Help me to turn from my sin and follow You.
Teach me what it means to walk in freedom as I live under Your grace,
and help me to grow in Your ways as I seek to know You more.
Amen.

If you just prayed this prayer (or something similar in your own words), would you email us at info@lovegodgreatly.com?

We'd love to help get you started on this exciting journey as a child of God!

WELCOME FRIEND

We're so glad you're here

Love God Greatly exists to inspire, encourage, and equip women all over the world to make God's Word a priority in their lives.

INSPIRE

women to make God's Word a priority in their daily lives through our Bible study resources.

ENCOURAGE

women in their daily walks with God through online community and personal accountability.

EQUIP

women to grow in their faith, so that they can effectively reach others for Christ.

Love God Greatly consists of a beautiful community of women who use a variety of technology platforms to keep each other accountable in God's Word.

We start with a simple Bible reading plan, but it doesn't stop there.

Some gather in homes and churches locally, while others connect online with women across the globe. Whatever the method, we lovingly lock arms and unite for this purpose...to Love God Greatly with our lives.

At Love God Greatly, you'll find real, authentic women. Women who are imperfect, yet forgiven. Women who desire less of us, and a whole lot more of Jesus. Women who long to know God through his Word, because we know that Truth transforms and sets us free. Women who are better together, saturated in God's Word and in community with one another.

Love God Greatly is a 501 (C) (3) non-profit organization. Funding for Love God Greatly comes through donations and proceeds from our online Bible study journals and books. LGG is committed to providing quality Bible study materials and believes finances should never get in the way of a woman being able to participate in one of our studies. All journals and translated journals are available to download for free from LoveGodGreatly.com for those who cannot afford to purchase them. Our journals and books are also available for sale on Amazon. Search for "Love God Greatly" to see all of our Bible study journals and books. 100% of proceeds go directly back into supporting Love God Greatly and helping us inspire, encourage and equip women all over the world with God's Word.

THANK YOU for partnering with us!

WHAT WE OFFER:

18 + Translations | Bible Reading Plans | Online Bible Study
Love God Greatly App | 80 + Countries Served
Bible Study Journals & Books | Community Groups

EACH LGG STUDY INCLUDES:

Three Devotional Corresponding Blog Posts
Memory Verses | Weekly Challenge | Weekly Reading Plan
Reflection Questions And More!

OTHER LOVE GOD GREATLY STUDIES INCLUDE:

Love the Loveless | Fear & Anxiety | James | His Name Is...
Philippians | 1 & 2 Timothy | Sold Out | Ruth | Broken & Redeemed
Walking in Wisdom | God With Us | In Everything Give Thanks
You Are Forgiven | David | Ecclesiastes | Growing Through Prayer
Names of God | Galatians | Psalm 119 | 1st & 2nd Peter
Made For Community | The Road To Christmas
The Source Of Gratitude | Esther | You Are Loved

Visit us online at

LOVEGODGREATLY.COM

Made in the USA
Lexington, KY
04 March 2019